For the New Board Member

For the New Board Member

An Orientation to Board Governance in the Not-for-Profit Sector

BRUCE A. RYAN
2017

ISBN: 1544072325
ISBN 13: 9781544072326
Library of Congress Control Number: 2017906392
CreateSpace Independent Publishing Platform
North Charleston, South Carolina

Contents

1

Setting the Context

So, YOU HAVE been asked to serve on the board of directors of a not-for-profit agency. What, you ask, are the responsibilities of a board member? There are many, and some of them are substantial. This is a commitment not to be taken lightly.

Serving on a board is an honor, and it offers you the opportunity to make a very valuable contribution to the workings of your community. However, you really should decline the invitation to serve if you cannot commit your time or if you plan to be absent from your community for extended periods, thus precluding a reasonable level of attendance at board or committee meetings. Many people, including agency clients, staff, and your fellow board members, will be looking to you for a meaningful contribution and effort.

However, if you are willing and ready, welcome aboard, and be prepared for a stimulating and rewarding experience.

The intent of this book is to provide an orientation to a useful way of thinking about board governance and the various roles often required of board members. It is not an in-depth discussion of the techniques of board governance or an analysis of governance theory, although it contains elements of both. My aim is to do what the title says: provide an orientation rather than an exhaustive education about board governance.

There is an almost infinite variety of ways for boards to govern, although the literature tends to converge on a small number of models or approaches. The Internet is replete with websites from consultancies that describe many variations on governance practices. Most of this literature comes in the form of tips and guides for practice. No one model or approach is absolutely correct. All of them have validity, and all of them can be done well or badly. Governing badly usually means that the chosen governance model's rules and guides are not being applied consistently or coherently. Boards and agencies generally stay out of governance difficulties when they stick with the policies and rules they have officially adopted, whatever they are.

There are many traps for boards and board members to fall into that needlessly and too often result in unproductive and even damaging actions. I believe that if board members can acquire a sound conception of the governance task (regardless of the governance model being used), they will be better equipped to avoid mistakes. Further, a good understanding of the governance task should improve the likelihood that board members will be able to contribute strongly and effectively to the operations of their agency. My hope is that a well-oriented board member will be better able to read and benefit from more extensive works concerned with governance theory and practice.

In my thirty-five years of serving on a variety of boards of directors and during my work as an accreditation reviewer for family-service agencies in Ontario and in a number of other Canadian provinces, I have seen a revolution in our understanding of appropriate board governance. Today, our appreciation of added board value is much more sophisticated than it was in the 1970s. In those earlier days, there was very little published advice for board members; one learned from the experienced hands on the board. The bylaws, along with the letters patent or articles of incorporation, were about the only written guidance available for board practice—but they offered, as is still the case today, little beyond the basic legal operating requirements as specified by the law pertaining to corporations. There is much more to board governance than what bylaws and other basic legal documents can possibly provide.

The ideas considered in this book are rather like a jigsaw puzzle. They all fit together in a coherent pattern that cannot be fully understood until the reader has worked his or her way to the final chapter. The different components in the governance process are highly interconnected. For example, the full significance of the distinction between accountability and responsibility really can't be grasped without understanding the importance of careful delegation of agency work from board to executive director. Further, the importance of work delegation is better understood after the reader addresses the task of operations monitoring in relation to board-defined strategic goals and values. In short, an understanding of governance cannot be gained piecemeal; each component is linked to all other components.

To reiterate, this short orientation offers a glimpse into the wider knowledge to be found in more in-depth books on governance. Resources providing some of this more extensive information can be found at the end of the book.

2

The Challenge of Governance

A N AGENCY BOARD of directors must not only govern; it must also understand why and how it carries out its governing responsibilities. In all my years of meeting boards of directors, I have found them much stronger at knowing about the governing practices they are following than they are at understanding why those practices either are or are not effective. This is not a surprise. There is a tendency in board orientation sessions to skip the topic of "governance as a challenge" in favor of "governance techniques." Yet these techniques are simply practices that have been developed over the years to deal with the challenges that naturally emerge for boards as they cope with the responsibilities that common and corporate law have assigned to them.

My view is that if board members make some initial effort to appreciate the problems of governance, they will be in a much better position to understand and use the techniques that countless consultants have recommended to boards. If board members grasp the issues that they must deal with as governors, then they will be in a much better position to select, use, and evaluate the variety of governance procedures available to them.

Therefore, before getting to a description of the key policy documents a board member should know about, let me spend some time exploring some key issues, concepts, and questions, in order to better understand governance as a challenging task, as opposed to a set of procedures or techniques.

Understanding Board Accountability and Responsibility

The notion of accountability is absolutely critical to any deeper grasp of what the duties and responsibilities of an agency's board of directors are.[1] In essence, clarifying accountability is the starting place for all board work, and all board members, whether new or experienced, need to understand this basic point.

I want to draw a distinction between what I am choosing to call *accountability* on the one hand and *responsibility* on the other. I intend to treat these terms as having different, although related, meanings while also acknowledging that any thesaurus will suggest that these terms are interchangeable in normal discourse. Of more importance is that there are two concepts that need to be clearly differentiated. I merely require words that can be attached to each of the two concepts to facilitate a discussion. I acknowledge that I am being somewhat arbitrary in my definitions.

In the context of my discussion, a person who is *accountable* for an action gets the credit or the blame for whatever the action achieves or fails to achieve. It does not matter if the person actually carries out the action; the person who is deemed ultimately accountable still gets the credit or blame, at least in the eyes of the world beyond the organization.

Being *responsible* for work means actually having to do the work. Responsibility for actions can be delegated to others, such as from board to chief executive officer (CEO)[2] or from the CEO to other staff

---

1 To whom the board is accountable is a separate issue. I deal with that question in chapter 3.

2 The traditional term of *executive director* has fallen out of favor; in recent years, there has been a strong trend in the not-for-profit sector to adopt the private sector's term of *CEO*.

members. The delegating party can, within its operational context, hold the delegatee accountable for the action and can exact a penalty if the delegatee fails to perform. This does not relieve the original delegating persons from their own ultimate accountability for whatever is done or not done.

Let's bring these ideas together in the board context. At the end of the day, the board is accountable for all actions in an agency. The board, however, is not directly responsible for carrying out all of those actions. The board's direct responsibilities are limited only to those actions that it does not delegate to agency staff or nonboard volunteers. Usually, the board delegates to the CEO all actions that it does not reserve for itself. Generally, these delegated responsibilities consist of administrative and service-delivery actions, those tasks that are typically referred to as *operational matters*.

In turn, the CEO can delegate responsibility for some administrative and service actions to senior managers who will, as appropriate, be held accountable by the CEO for those delegated responsibilities. So it goes, down through the organization, ending with frontline staff (or sometimes service volunteers) who have their own set of responsibilities for which they can be held accountable by the superior to whom they report. In the final analysis, however, the board can be held accountable for all actions, even though the board may have delegated responsibility for them to staff.

Clearly, if a board is held accountable for all agency actions and if it also takes steps to delegate responsibility for some of those actions to staff members, the board must protect itself by maintaining careful oversight of agency operations. The secret to effective and wise governance is to first find the best way to delegate and then ensure that the delegatees are carrying out appropriate actions. Failure to monitor delegatee actions invites accusations of board negligence, and doing it badly can precipitate a staff crisis. Do it well, and the result is an effective organization.

Accountability and Responsibility for What?

The core questions for all new board members revolve around understanding for what they will be held accountable and for what they will be responsible. The answer with respect to accountability is easy enough. As I have said, the board is ultimately accountable for all agency activities. It does not matter if the board has delegated the responsibility for actions to the staff through the CEO; in the end, the board remains accountable for everything.

The question of "responsibility for what" is more complex and nuanced. To deal adequately with the issue of whose responsibility is what, we need to tease apart the two main varieties of work that encompass the full spectrum of agency activity: governance work and operations work. All *governance work* must remain the responsibility of the board; it cannot be delegated to agency staff or to nonboard agency volunteers. In contrast, responsibility for *operations work*, usually defined as agency administrative and service-delivery activity, is normally and mostly delegated to the CEO, who may, in turn, delegate some of it to the staff.

Let's deal with governance work first. The activities that constitute governance work, the responsibility of the board, can be further divided into two different types of activity: policymaking work and governance-administration work. The policymaking category includes the creation of written statements concerning the agency's vision, mission, values, and service outcomes or strategic goals. This category also includes a range of policy statements concerning the board's own approach to governance and a description of the relationship between the board and its community on the one hand and with the staff on the other.

Activities in the governance-administration category include board education, monitoring of the agency's success in achieving its stated strategic goals, monitoring the agency's operational practices to ensure their consistency with board policies, monitoring the board's own work as a governing body, and evaluating the performance of the CEO. Clearly, there is plenty of governance work for boards to do.

Now, let's go back to operations work briefly. Why is operations work typically delegated to the CEO? The most important reason for delegation is that the CEO and the CEO's executive staff are the persons most professionally and technically competent to do the work. In a well-functioning organization, the work should be the responsibility of the most-qualified people. That said, the board does have the right, if it so wishes, to direct very strongly how the work is to be done; boards are, after all, held accountable for such work. The wise board will try to avoid retaining responsibility for operations work when that work really should be delegated to the people best trained to do it.

It is this power of boards to retain or delegate operations work that introduces complexity and nuance into the situation. Depending on the board and the level of sophistication of the staff or service volunteers who carry out the operations work, the board may decide to retain responsibility for certain activities such as check signing or approvals of certain kinds of expenditures. In short, not all operations can be delegated. I will return to this issue later because confusion in how this is done can be seriously damaging to agency functioning.

It would be a mistake to assume that because a board may delegate responsibility for operations work to staff, it also means that board members have no role in operational matters. Indeed, it is probably wise for staff to welcome board members to the table when operational planning is being considered. Board advice on how best to do things can be very useful—and often is, but if the responsibility for operations is to reside with the staff, they must be allowed to take or leave board advice. If, in the end, the staff make poor choices, they can be held accountable by the board and be subject to whatever sanctions the board deems appropriate. If the board insists or requires the staff to take and implement the board's advice, then the staff cannot be held accountable for the operational failures resulting from that advice (unless the staff clearly fail to implement the advice properly). Just how the board deals with this issue marks the difference between an effective and an ineffective board.

The key point here is that it is the type of work (governance or operations) that is of more importance than who does it. Who gets to do the work depends entirely on the decisions the board makes with respect to the delegation of responsibility. Clearly, it is critical that the board makes such decisions carefully and then acts prudently to ensure that those to whom the work has been delegated are left free to actually do the work and are also held accountable for their actions within the context of the agency. Even if the board is not actively managing the operations work the CEO and staff are doing, the board needs to know about the work and monitor what is being achieved.

Is It the Same for All Types of Boards?

At this point, it is usual to ask if it is appropriate to so firmly align governance work with the board and operations work with staff for all agencies. Some small agencies have no staff; all services are delivered through volunteers. At best, they might have a single staff member whose job is largely concerned with the coordination of service volunteers while also carrying out some other administrative responsibilities. It is obvious that the board/governance vs. staff/operations split works well for the large agency with highly trained professional staff, but what about the small, mainly volunteer-staffed organization? Sometimes it is said that John Carver's Policy Governance model[3] (which pushes strongly for this split) is appropriate for larger agencies with professional staff, while for smaller agencies, a simpler and more relaxed or traditional model is better, but is this really the case?

In my view, it is not helpful to think in terms of types of boards and agencies such as Policy Governance vs. traditional or modified policy

---

3 John Carver, *Boards That Make a Difference: A New Design for Leadership in Nonprofit and Public Organizations* (San Francisco: Jossey-Bass, 2006). The phrase, Policy Governance, has been trademarked by John Carver to identify his particular approach to board governance.

governance, these being the most frequently encountered terms these days. Instead, I see a long continuum of variations in board and agency characteristics, with the large agency and its very professional staff at one end and the small agency with board-member-delivered services at the other end. Nevertheless, no matter the nature of the agency, the issues of governance and operations remain, and each must be respected as different sorts of work.

Even in the board-member-run agency, there are the normal governance responsibilities that involve matters of strategic goal definition and overall policy development. The members of the board do this work wearing their board-member hats. The next day, these same persons might return to the agency as volunteers ready to do the service work of the agency, whether it be answering the telephone, typing up letters, or delivering whatever service the agency delivers. In doing this service work, they are wearing their service-volunteer hats. It is important that these volunteering persons keep their two roles and two types of work separate in order to avoid role confusion.

It is not helpful in the longer run if board-governance work is being done on the fly by individual board members who happen to be acting in their service-volunteer roles. Dual roles such as this are invariably difficult to navigate. It is critical that those involved in these tricky situations are constantly mindful of who they are at the moment (board member or service volunteer) and what work they are doing (governance or operations). If board members acting in their nonboard volunteer roles suddenly start implementing governance-policy changes, a great deal of organizational confusion will result.

So, my answer to the question is that it does not matter all that much what sort of board and agency is involved. The challenges of governance work on the one hand and operations work on the other remain important, and both must be dealt with carefully. The biggest challenge for volunteers on the board who delegate operational matters to other volunteers who carry out administrative or service functions (when there is no staff to be made responsible and held accountable) is that the board has little formal disciplinary power over the service volunteers when things do not go well. In these circumstances, skill in interpersonal relationships is critical.

With these basic concepts and issues out of the way, let me turn next to some important components of the board's governance work.

3

Defining Agency Purposes and Developing Board Policies

BEFORE THE BOARD begins to address the issues of responsibility delegation and the nature of agency operations, it has a very large set of policy-oriented tasks to complete. The board must first define what the agency is supposed to achieve in the community and then develop a range of rules or policies that guide board conduct. For the majority of people who join a board, most of this sort of work has already been done or should have been done. It is the new board member's responsibility to learn about and understand agency purposes and governance practices. It is also important that boards offer an effective board-orientation program to new board members.

In Whose Interests?

One of the first things a new board member needs to learn is in whose interests is the agency/organization is acting. The board must be able to describe the community of persons that is to ultimately benefit from the agency's services. Clarifying the in-whose-interests question is important because the answer identifies the population being represented by the members of the board of directors and to which the board is accountable.

Developing such a description is not an easy task; many agencies do not do it. A very common practice is to formulate statements for vision, mission, and values and hope that the ground is covered. While such vision and mission statements might indeed contain reference to a community, in most cases the definition of the board-represented community is left troublingly vague. At some point, the board needs to articulate a strategic purpose for the organization, and this task is greatly simplified if the board has a clear-eyed sense of who and what is to benefit from the organization's work.

One place for boards to start in this task of defining the represented community—those John Carver termed the *moral owners*[4]—is to identify the stakeholders and see if they can be deemed the ultimate beneficiaries of the agency's services. Staff members obviously constitute a key set of stakeholders, but it makes little sense to think of them as beneficiaries of the proffered services outside of the incomes they earn and the social relationships they gain from the workplace; agencies do not offer services so that their staffs can be paid and lead productive lives.

Boards of directors are typically elected at an annual general meeting of the organization, as defined in the agency bylaws. Agency members as electors could be seen as the "owners," although most members or directors are not typically direct beneficiaries of agency services. Besides, it is increasingly common for not-for-profit organizations to restrict the definition of "members" to only the persons who sit on the board of directors. As part of the community population, however, it can

---

4 Some object to the term "owners" in this context because the persons being referred to are not owners in the sense that they have paid any money to become owners in the traditional sense. The objectors have a point. To ease the complexity of language in this section, I have employed Carver's terminology but have placed quotation marks around the term to acknowledge the term's somewhat ironic use herein.

be claimed that they benefit from the overall community improvement that comes from the agency providing its services.

Clients, on the other hand, clearly benefit from services. As such, they should be seen as part of the "owner" group—but that is not the whole of the story. Normally, when agency boards of directors make submissions to funders for financial support, they make wider claims and argue that the community as a whole will benefit when the agency's services are available to an identified client population. This suggests that the board might extend its vision and think of the whole community as the body of people for whom the board members are acting as representatives.

At the same time, there needs to be a sensible limit on how widely board visioning should extend. The intended service reach of the agency is a key consideration. If the organization is a neighborhood group, it is likely to restrict the ownership group to the people who live in the relevant neighborhood. If the agency is offering its services to any person in need who lives within the city boundaries, then it makes sense to define the entire city population as the ownership group.

Why bother with worrying about the community for whom the board acts? Is there any practical benefit to defining such a group? In fact, several benefits flow from being clear about an agency's community of "owners". First, in developing its strategic goals (a key task of the board), it is important for the board to understand the nature of the community from which the agency's clients come. Clients do not live in isolation. They are a part of a social network that offers supports while also contributing to the challenges its clients face. Appreciating these community-level impacts on clients helps the board clarify the nature of the services to be offered and the strategic goals to be achieved. Service priorities can then be more confidently set.

Second, agency clients rarely receive services from a single agency. In almost all cases, at least one other service is actively serving client needs; multiple-agency involvement is not unusual. The difficulties people face are typically multidimensional and arise from more than a single cause.

Working with other agencies and professionals is now the service norm. Being careful about defining the community of "owners" increases the likelihood that other service providers will be explicitly seen as part of the community's human-service system. Increased interagency collaboration in meeting the needs of clients is a more likely consequence.

Third, when it is time for the board to report on its accomplishments to its community, which should be at least an annual event, the task is made easier and the communication more effective if the board knows clearly to whom it is reporting. When the board's relationship to its "owner" community is clearly perceived, the board is more likely to appreciate what the ownership needs to know about the agency's services.

Determining Agency Purposes

One of the most important governance responsibilities that boards have, and one they cannot delegate, is specifying what the agency is supposed to achieve in the community. This is a major task that is arguably more challenging and more serious than anything else a board might wish to do. In declaring that the agency is to achieve certain major strategic service goals, the board is informing the staff and service volunteers about what is expected from them. Figuring out the agency's strategic goals is complicated. It occurs at multiple levels in the organization and involves both board and staff working together with varying degrees of intensity, depending on which components of strategy are being emphasized at any given time.

I feel the need to digress briefly here. The language involved in defining agency purpose can quickly become confusing. John Carver, after considerable experience in working with agency boards, decided to use the term, *Ends*[5] to designate the key component of strategic thinking that should occupy the board. Ends, in Carver's approach, refer to the

---

5 In the context of discussions about Carver's Policy Governance approach, the words Ends and Means have technical meanings and are generally written with the initial letter capitalized.

impacts or effects that agency services have on clients or the community. They describe what difference is made as a result of the agency delivering its services.

Those new to governance often don't feel comfortable with Carver's Ends language and seem to prefer other more conventional terms such as *goals*. However, words like *goals* and *objectives* tend to lead to confusing descriptions of hierarchies, with goals seen as more general than objectives and so on. In consideration of those uncomfortable with Ends, I have chosen to employ the phrase *strategic goals*, but I intend the term to mean the same thing as Carver's Ends. I am hoping that by calling the goals of focus here strategic goals, readers will find the language easier to accept. Nonetheless, Carver's warning is valid, and we need to remain mindful of being distracted by red herrings. The board's focus should be clearly on the client or community outcomes that the agency's services should produce. End of digression.

Chait, Ryan, and Taylor (2004)[6] employed the term *generative governance* to designate this critical aspect of board work. In developing agency's strategic goals/Ends, board members must bring together their collective knowledge of the community, its needs, and its strengths. This information must be combined with the best advice on service delivery that is available from key professionals and experts in the field. Staff members who have been hired to deliver those services typically provide such advice, but it might also come from outside sources. While board members certainly bring community knowledge to the process, they don't usually have all the expertise needed in the professions relevant to their agency.

What strategic elements will a board develop through this generative process? Today, virtually all agencies will have a set of vision, mission, and values statements. They are intended to capture the sense of

---

6 R. P. Chait, W. P. Ryan, and B. E. Taylor, *Governance as Leadership: Reframing the Work of Nonprofit Boards* (Hoboken, NJ: John Wiley & Sons, 2004).

purpose and general manner of operation that the board sees for its organization. These statements function as guides to both the board and the staff as the latter develop their administrative and service operations. Operational proposals can be evaluated against the vision, mission, and values statements, thereby creating cohesion and consistency in agency functioning. At least, that is the theory.

As far as defining strategic goals/Ends goes, the problem with nearly all vision, mission, and values statements is that they don't go far enough or provide the level of detail that a CEO can use to productively guide the workings of the agency. Generally, they are expressed in highly abstract language and are, by design, brief and pithy. Like poetry, they are intended to capture essence. In reality, both board and staff need more than that to guide them in formulating ways to deliver agency services. The solution to this problem is the strategic-planning process.

These days, many (if not most) boards set aside a retreat day each year. They work with their senior staff to develop a new strategic plan or review and modify a previously developed plan. This plan, so developed or reviewed and modified, is then often presented to the full board for approval at its next scheduled regular meeting. The board-approved plan becomes the key set of instructions directing the service delivery or operations work done by staff or service volunteers. However, this traditional approach to strategic planning by boards has a number of conceptual and procedural problems associated with it. I will turn to these problems in due course, but before I do that, however, we need to clarify some important concepts.

The strategic-planning process has two important components that can (and probably should) be dealt with separately. The first component is concerned with defining strategic goals or Carver's Ends. The second component is the creation of what amounts to an operational plan that lays out what service-delivery and administrative steps the staff or service volunteers will take to achieve the strategic goals/Ends; Carver refers to these as *Means*. Dealing with these separate parts of a total strategy process involves different kinds of expertise and awareness. Establishing strategic goals/Ends requires knowledge of the community's characteristics, needs, and social features. Such considerations are clearly within the responsibility of the board, and determining what the agency's services should achieve in the community is a task that rightly belongs to the board, which, presumably, has been adequately educated for the task.

Dealing with the question of how to deliver the services that will achieve the strategic goals/Ends usually requires professional and service knowledge that is not normally held by board members. Instead, the board almost always turns to the staff for advice on the best way to achieve the board-determined strategic goals for the agency. Just how boards use this professional knowledge in the agency's planning process and how they decide to assign responsibility for the planning task has significant implications for how accountability is distributed within the organization. In Carver's terms, we should be careful about how we assign responsibility for the development of Ends and the conduct of Means.

Defining Strategic Goals or Ends

Let's step back to the part of the strategy process that unambiguously belongs to the board: defining strategic goals/Ends. Such goals offer a description of what should be achieved by the delivery of agency services. A well-articulated set of strategic goal/Ends statements provides clear guidance to staff as they develop the appropriate service-delivery mechanisms. At the same time, this also provides a reasonable basis on which to develop useful methods for assessing service effectiveness.

The key to devising useful strategic goal/Ends statements is to employ language that describes outcomes or impact effects rather than service-process terminology. Process terms too easily lead to descriptions of the services to be delivered instead of the results that should follow from the delivery of those services. A few examples:

Process Language

- "The agency will provide parent-education programs for single-parent families."
- "The agency will provide credit-counseling services for individuals to help prevent them from going into personal bankruptcy."

Outcomes Language

- "Parents will be better able to cope with their children's behavior problems."
- "The number of individuals applying for personal bankruptcy in the community will be reduced."

It is tempting to say that I am being unduly fussy about terminology and too picky with wording. While that might be the case, the way we describe things tends to determine reality for us. If goal statements use process language, board members tend to focus attention on the services being delivered and not on what good (or lack thereof) the services are doing. If the board requires that staff develop indicators of service success and has used process language in its strategic goal/Ends statements, then the staff will be more likely to report on service-process indicators. They may, for example, report on how many parent-education programs they offered and how many hours of credit counseling were delivered. If, instead, outcomes language is used, the board will tend to look for staff reports on service impacts. It will ask for data to show, for example, that parents are being more effective in dealing with their children or that the numbers of personal bankruptcies are actually going down.

Too often boards, in their strategic-planning retreats, give too little time to or simply skip over the strategic goal/Ends definition work and focus strongly on service delivery. The result is most often a specified set of services that are to be provided by staff. Missing is the declaration of what the services are intended to achieve for clients or the community. Again, what we call our task has a big impact on what we think we are doing. If we call it strategic planning, we will make a plan. If we call it strategic goal/Ends setting, we will be more likely to focus on strategic goals/Ends.

How, then, does a board go about developing effective strategic goal/Ends statements? For many agencies that have been in operation for a number of years, these statements are already implicit in their existing strategic plans and service-delivery practices. Often, they are hidden in one form or another in the contracts they sign with funders. In these situations, the board members should ask themselves what impacts they think their agency services, as currently delivered, should be having, and simply write them down. More often than not, the very act of making them explicit will lead to new insights into what the agency might better be working toward. The effort invariably gives the board and the staff a stronger focus on the task of determining whether they are indeed adding real value to their community.

Whether it is making explicit those strategic goals/Ends that are already implicit or generating entirely new ones, the challenge for the board is not so different. Performing this sort of board work requires the marshaling of community knowledge, information about client needs, and an evaluation of the agency's capacity to deliver the kinds of services required to achieve the goals. A board cannot do this job unless it is well engaged with the community, knows its needs, is aware of what other agencies are doing in the community, and is being kept informed of service-delivery best practices. The board must create ways of having information flow to it in the form of board education, and it must adequately monitor how well and to what effect the agency's services are being delivered. If, at the end of the day, the board is held accountable, it must constantly assure itself that the services offered to the clients are achieving the strategic goals/Ends articulated in their policy statements.

Boards should not try to develop strategic goals/Ends on their own, and while it is critical to gather information from outside sources, boards must work closely with staff in developing their goal statements. Chait, Ryan, and Taylor (2005) make a very strong case for a joint board/staff effort for important strategic work. In the end, however, it should be understood by both board and staff that the strategic goal/Ends products of this joint process are the responsibility of the board. The strategic goal/Ends statements must receive formal board approval, and the board must accept full accountability for their content, even though it receives staff advice in the process.

How Detailed Should the Strategic Goals/Ends Be?

One of the major challenges a board faces when formulating its strategic goals/Ends is determining how specific to make them. Clearly, they can be stated at a very broad and general level such as, "Clients will be better able to deal with life's challenges." While this wording clearly satisfies the requirement that goals be stated as client outcomes, it does not provide much direction for what particular outcomes the staff should be aiming to achieve. More specificity is likely in order.

For example, if the agency is a family-counseling service, the board might further define this very general goal as "Clients who are married and have children will be more successful in their marital relationships and will become more effective parents." Taking it further, the board might also ask that "Client couples will report more harmonious relationships." Further service-goal specification might be that client couples "will report more satisfying sexual relationships" and that "conflicts/fights between partners will be reduced in frequency and intensity." Just where should this detailing of strategic goals/Ends stop?

Carver's advice here is helpful. He recommends that boards begin stating their strategic goals/Ends at the most general level and then increase the degree of specificity and detail until they reach a point where they can accept "any reasonable interpretation" from the CEO of the more generally stated service outcomes. The board's work will create a document containing strategic goal/Ends statements that comprise a set of nested statements that range from the more abstract and general down to something more specific, detailed, and concrete. Typically, however, the board's degree of specificity will remain more abstract and general than what the staff eventually requires in order to focus its service planning. At this point, the CEO will be expected to take the board's least-general statements and then define even more specific service outcomes that are consistent with the board's higher-level statements. The board, of course, will have to declare that it is satisfied with the CEO's reasonable interpretation of the board's higher-level statements when the finer grained and more specific outcomes are defined at the staff level. If the board is not satisfied, it will either have to tell the CEO to try again, or it will have to re-state the higher-level strategic goals/Ends so that the CEO can work with them.

To iterate, the board will prepare its strategic goal/Ends statements by first setting them out in highly abstract and general language. They can then write a number of more specific strategic goals/Ends in progressively more focused language until they feel it has gone far enough to give the CEO a fairly clear picture of what the board thinks should be achieved as a result of agency services. The board stops at this point and invites the CEO to interpret reasonably what the board is seeking when defining fully concrete and measurable outcome indicators. A desirable consequence of this process is that the board will automatically have in hand a useful set of tools for monitoring agency effectiveness. I will return to this issue in chapter 5.

So Much for the Strategic Goals; What about the Strategic Plan?

Earlier I argued that it is useful to separate the task of *defining* strategic goals/Ends from the business of formulating a plan to *achieve* the goals/Ends. The former is clearly a board responsibility and an essential part of the board's governance work. The plan, however, is basically a description of what the agency will be doing to ensure that the goals/ Ends are achieved. The plan is a description of operations, direct service, and administrative procedures. Typically, the board has delegated these matters to the CEO and the staff. Thus, the development of the service-delivery plan is operational work that more properly belongs to the CEO. I will return to the issue of the board's role in developing the plan in the next chapter.

What about Values?

So far, I have repeatedly listed the typical big-three products of board-governance work: vision, mission, and values. Vision and mission usually find expression in one way or another in the definition of strategic goals and in the strategic plan, whether or not the plan is developed by the board or by the staff, but what about values?

For the most part, any list of agency values (e.g., honesty, openness, accessibility, fairness, trust, respect, supportiveness, inclusion) consists of terms that describe how people should be treated. As such, they are more concerned with the way the work should be done, in contrast to what the work will achieve. With respect to governance work, the agency's approved values will be expressed in the policies focused on the board's approach to governance practices. Values-oriented language, for example, is typically found in board codes of conduct and in policy-level statements providing guidance on how board meetings or annual general meetings should be conducted.

Another key place where the agency value statements play an important role in is the language used in the policy documents developed to define the responsibilities delegated to the CEO. The CEO, for example, might be instructed to ensure that the agency is operated in an open and transparent manner, and that staff, clients, and volunteers are treated fairly and with respect. Further, operational policies will be developed to require that staff to treat each other and their clients similarly.

It is sometimes tempting to see values as strategic goals/Ends. For example, it seems very important to deliver a service honestly and in an accessible manner and to be open to feedback and criticism. Surely, these values are worthy goals. You will recall that discussion a couple of pages back where I referred to Carver's concern about using the term *goals* instead of *Ends*. We are indeed on the edge of a quagmire here. The point I am trying to make is that Ends (or *strategic* goals) refer to outcome effects on agency clients due to agency services and that vision and mission statements usually point to such outcomes (the agency's strategic goals or Ends). In contrast, values statements almost always point to the way service is delivered, such that the strategic goals/Ends are effectively and properly achieved. As such, values statements are al-most always linked to service *processes* rather than *outcomes*.

Sustaining Unity in the Board's Voice

Whenever the board speaks of the agency's "vision and mission" (or about anything else, for that matter), it should do so with a single, uni-fied voice. Whether communications from the board are directed exter-nally to the community or internally to the staff, volunteers, and agency clients, the message must be coherent and consistent with board-estab-lished values and policies. Of course, boards should be developing their strategic positions in the context of healthy debate and the productive questioning of relevant information and options. However, when mat-ters are resolved either through consensus or via a majority vote, all board members must be prepared to stick to the message.

Divergent views coming from a board can be damaging. To those outside the agency, inconsistent messaging undermines the community's understanding of what the agency intends to accomplish. Funders can become confused and reluctant to support agency operations. Potential clients become uncertain about what services to expect. Perhaps the most significant damage, however, can be internal. A fractured voice from the board is not helpful to the staff in general and particularly to the CEO, who must direct the work of the staff and motivate them to work hard toward achieving the board-defined strategic goals/Ends.

Managing the Board's Business

Years ago, often the only written policy document that guided boards in the conduct of their work as governing entities was their organization's bylaws. Traditionally, bylaws have specified the legally binding actions required of incorporated not-for-profit agencies with respect to the holding of annual general meetings, the election of board members (directors), the subsequent election of officers, and the establishment of the board's standing committees. The bylaws typically, but not always, set director term limits and ensure the steady and gradual turnover of directors.

What the traditional bylaws did not do was define the way the board was to conduct its business during and between regular board meetings. Instead, boards tended to follow unwritten rules of practice that have evolved generally within the not-for-profit sector and, more particularly, within the culture of each agency and which were handed down to succeeding generations of boards. In a rough sort of way, this tradition worked pretty well, and a positive relationship between board and agency staff would usually permit the organization to carry out the agency's business effectively and productively. Too often, though, this rather loose approach to board business rules would lead boards into conflict with staff-level decisions, thereby undermining management authority. The lack of clarity concerning when and how the board should intervene made it difficult for both sides.

Today, however, boards must operate with a much higher degree of self-consciousness and self-critical discipline. Boards need to be mindful in their approach to governance work. They should develop written statements to guide their actions, and they should develop self-assessment tools that, if honestly used, will give them constructive feedback on how well they are adhering to their own written rules or governance policies.

There are no hard-and-fast rules about the kinds of written guides a board would be wise to develop and adopt. Remember, these written policy statements are nothing special in and of themselves; they are merely tools and devices the board can use to guide its way through its governance responsibilities. John Carver has written extensively on the wisdom of such a formal approach to board business management, and his book *Boards That Make a Difference: A New Design for Leadership in Nonprofit and Public Organizations*[7] contains many ideas and examples of useful board management policy statements. Among the most significant are policies respecting:

- **The relationship between the agency and its community.** In this statement, the board defines the community of "owners" it seeks to represent, commits itself to informing itself of the community, and specifies how it intends to communicate with and report back to the community.
- **The definition of the agency's strategic goals/Ends.** Along with the usual specification of agency vision, mission, and values, this is one of the most important responsibilities of any agency board. Such strategic goal/Ends statements clarify for the staff and the community what the agency intends to achieve for its clients and the wider community.
- **The board's general approach to governance.** Here, the board outlines in general terms how it intends to conduct its business. It spells out how board members should treat each other. Further, it commits itself to a rigorous analysis of its own functioning and also to a careful monitoring of all agency operations, in order to

---

7 John Carver. *Boards That Make a Difference: A New Design for Leadership in Nonprofit and Public Organizations* (San Francisco: Jossey-Bass, 2006).

ensure the achievement of its strategic goals/Ends, particularly those that might pose a risk for the agency.

- **Board member code of conduct.** While it is now almost universally practiced that agencies develop and adopt a code of conduct expected of staff and volunteers, the adoption of a parallel code respecting board members in their governance role is less common. Certainly, board-member codes will include the usual guidance respecting conflicts of interest and self-dealing that all staff and volunteers are expected to follow, but a board-specific code will also explicitly commit the board members to representing the interests of the community of "owners" and warn board members against any attempt to exert individual authority over any aspect of the organization.

- **Board responsibilities.** In contrast to the more general statement on the board's approach to governance, the list of board responsibilities is more specific. The list need not be long and detailed, but it should identify the key governance tasks for which the board must be responsible, including what policies are to be developed, adopted, and then reviewed at specified intervals; which and to what extent, if any, staff-operational plans are to be reviewed; the approval of the annual budget, if they decide to retain that responsibility, and any other document as required by funders; and finally how and when the performance of the CEO will be reviewed in relation to specified performance criteria.

- **Chairperson's role.** The board chair plays a particularly critical role in board leadership. The chair has traditionally been the key board spokesperson on matters public, and the board depends on the board chair to ensure the smooth running of board meetings. In addition, the board chair is expected to show strategic leadership and see to it that the board remains faithful to its approach to governance and in the unification of its voice to instruct the CEO how he or she must operate to achieve the agency's board-defined strategic goals/Ends. The chairperson's role statement also should limit the individual authority of the chairperson to prevent him or her from claiming any special position of supervision over the CEO.

Beyond these policy statements that a wise board will adopt, there remain those policies concerned with the delegation of operational responsibility and the specification of how the CEO and the staff will pursue those delegated responsibilities. If the relationship between the board and the staff fractures, it is almost invariably because something has gone wrong with respect to the way delegated responsibilities are handled either by the board or by the CEO. Clarity in the conditions of delegation is extremely helpful. Delegation policies should be developed carefully and with the full participation of the CEO. The issues involved in delegating responsibility for operations work are addressed in the next chapter.

4

Delegating Responsibility

WE NOW COME to the place where agency work gets complicated and potentially very troublesome for both boards and CEOs. At this point, boards can unknowingly sow the seeds for problems in their relationship with the CEO/staff if they are not careful in dealing with the responsibilities they have delegated to the CEO. With careful planning and a clear vision of what they are doing and why they are doing it, boards can create the conditions that will release the full professional expertise of their CEO and staff members.

Ironically, the issue might be more complicated now than it was thirty or more years ago, when boards tended to assume they could act freely in operational matters and CEOs simply understood that this was the reality of working in the not-for-profit sector. Successful CEOs became proficient at how they managed board involvement and learned how to control their boards deftly. In a sense, boards could do and did anything they wanted to do at any time they wanted to do it, but sophisticated CEOs ensured that the board only wanted to do whatever the CEO wanted them to do. In these ways, a clever CEO could make the board feel powerful. For the most part, these fluid, dynamic relationships between boards and CEOs worked reasonably well. The situation, however, presented many opportunities for significant damage to agencies, and many agencies did get into trouble because of splits between the board and the CEO. In the face of such difficulties, board-governance theory and practice has evolved to prevent board/staff conflicts from becoming seriously destructive.

Why Assigning Clear Work Roles to Board and Staff Does Not Always Help

Much of the credit for the move toward more clarity in the assignment of board and staff work responsibilities within an agency context goes to John Carver who, in the 1970s, began working with boards that had come to grief in board/staff relationships. His diagnosis at the time was that board members were spending too much of their time doing what the CEO and the staff should be doing and too little time engaging in matters of larger strategy and linkages with the community. As Jim Doyle[8] has noted, by the middle 1990s, Carver's impact on the field of governance was major. Boards across the world were busy incorporating his theory of Policy Governance into their board practices.

By the end of the 1990s, however, one frequently heard of boards who had adopted the Carver Model, who then found themselves in various kinds of messes that generally stemmed from their lack of awareness of what their CEO and staff were actually doing. Having been so educated by their CEOs, some boards believed that operational matters were not their business, so they ceased asking questions about such issues, including (astonishingly enough) financial matters. In some cases, boards claimed shock and surprise over how staff were delivering services. Occasionally and more seriously, boards discovered that key members of staff had engaged in fraud and had siphoned off significant amounts of money from agency accounts. As stories of this sort

---

8 Jim Doyle, *The Elements of Effective Board Governance* (Washington, DC: Community College Press, 2009).

emerged, doubts about the wisdom of following what they understood to be Carver's advice began to spread.

Indeed, some boards became reluctant to begin using Carver's ideas; some moved back to a version of governance they termed "modified Carver" but which actually abandoned Carver entirely (even though they often retained some of his language in their policies). Such boards and agencies are simply operating within the long tradition of not-for-profits where the board dipped in and out of operational matters and the CEOs managed the somewhat-unpredictable board involvement with relative equanimity, as CEOs have always done.

My work as an accreditation on-site reviewer has brought me into contact with many boards and agencies that have become reluctant to follow Carver's advice. From my perspective, the difficulty for boards with Carver's approach is that it requires a good deal of study to understand it, even though in reality, the principles upon which it is based are few in number and simple to keep in mind. It does require rigorous discipline in following through on what Carver's theory suggests as best practice.

Too often, boards will hire a consultant to come into the agency to work with board and staff to implement the Policy Governance model. The appropriate governance policies will be drafted by the consultant and presented to the board for approval. Approvals are given, although frequently boards have a remarkably shallow grasp of why the policy language is the way it is, even though most Policy Governance consultants will try very hard to get board members to understand.

When the consultant leaves, the board will have a clear set of policy statements that tell them what to do and how to do it, but these documents then often tend to get treated in one of two different ways. Sometimes the policy statements are put into a policy binder and filed away, never to be seen again. Other times, the policy statements are regarded as rulebooks that they feel should be followed to the letter. However, agency realities are not normally conducive to mere rule following; there are invariably situations where the rules have to be thoughtfully interpreted rather than simply followed. To interpret thoughtfully, one must understand the principles behind the policy documents, and this requires effort. Too often, neither the board nor the CEO will invest the time and energy to complete the task.

Carver's warning to boards about ultimate accountability can be forgotten by both board and CEO, with the latter sometimes getting into turf warfare with the board over who is to know about or be involved in what. This is where the advantages of both the old and new approaches to governance have been lost. What we see is the worst of both worlds.

None of this is what Carver intended. His purpose was not to provide a rigid set of rules or governance techniques that were to be slavishly followed. Carver argues that his is a theory of governance, a way of thinking about governance that will help clarify the various roles of board and staff in the context of agency work and activity. The model policies and rules of thumb that populate his books are offered as illustrations of what boards might decide to do, but he makes it clear that boards are to think their own way through the governance challenges using a few first principles.

The point here is that simply clarifying roles is only part of the story. After the different board and CEO roles have been clarified through the delegation of responsibilities, the board still has a considerable amount of work to do. I will come back to a discussion of this additional work in the next chapter.

By What Means Does the Board Delegate Responsibilities to the CEO?

In general, responsibility delegation by the board takes one of two forms: *prescription* or *proscription*. When a board develops a job description as the key vehicle that instructs the CEO on his or her duties, it is prescribing the many actions that the CEO is expected to take. Traditionally, this has been the usual approach to the delegation of responsibilities.

More recently, however, an increasing number of boards are following Carver's recommendation that they use a proscriptive approach, wherein the board specifies the relatively few actions the CEO is *not* to take, while also stating that the CEO may take any other administrative and professional actions, as long as they lead to the achievement of the agency's strategic goals/Ends. Both approaches come with their challenges, which every board member should understand and appreciate. Let's look at the two delegation strategies one at a time.

Pursuing a Prescriptive Strategy

Of these two options, the prescriptive strategy using the traditional job description is the most easily understood. Today, virtually all agencies have descriptions for the various positions within the organization. There is, however, only one job description for which the board must retain responsibility: that of the CEO. All the rest can be left to the CEO to develop and implement, although if they wish to retain such an operational role, board members can have a hand in developing and approving all job descriptions. For a variety of reasons, this might not be the wisest course of action, but it is within the board's power to do it.

Traditional job descriptions for CEOs (and any other organization position) offer two important and powerful benefits. They provide a general but easily understandable account of what the CEO's job entails. They also offer a very useful and essential tool in CEO recruitment, where potential candidates must have a reasonable idea of what the job will require of them.

On the other hand, traditional job descriptions can be problematic, in a couple of ways. First, because the language in job descriptions is explicitly prescriptive, the implication is that the board is free to tell the CEO, in reasonably precise terms, how that person should be doing the job. Unless the board is very mindful of its governance work, it might find itself taking over responsibilities for operational work that it originally intended to delegate to the CEO. It is not the case that job descriptions *cause* the board to move more strongly into operations than it might wish; the problem is that the language might make it harder to detect board/CEO boundaries.

The second and more significant difficulty with the job description as a delegation device arises from the fact that all CEO operational activity cannot be included in a job description. A CEO is typically a professional with advanced levels of training and with the responsibility for a complex organization that provides commensurately complex professional services. In this situation, the CEO will make many decisions and take many actions. Only a relative handful of these different decisions and actions can be explicitly identified in a job description, otherwise the list of duties will become impossibly long. Often, these extra duties are covered by the catchall phrase, "and whatever other duties the board may assign."

Why is this a problem? The difficulty arises because prescriptive language can suggest that a CEO should only do what the board says the CEO should do. The implication is that a CEO action is legitimate only if it is so authorized in the job description. The status of any action not listed in the job description can be ambiguous. If the action is not listed but is obviously trivial, both board and CEO will likely understand that it is reasonable for the CEO to take it without seeking board approval. No problem there.

Sometimes, however, an action might be seem to be trivial on the surface. As such, it might not warrant inclusion in a job description yet have significant consequences. What should a CEO do in this case? If the board is in a generous frame of mind and relationships between board and CEO are good, the CEO can probably act without hesitation—but that might not always be the case. Just to be safe, for example, the CEO might bring the matter to the board for approval, which pulls the board into operational work. A CEO might choose to take action without mentioning it to the board, after which the board might decide the CEO should have secured board approval first. Ambiguity of this sort can be highly problematic.

Pursuing a Proscriptive Strategy

Over the last few decades, Carver has encouraged boards to avoid the delegation ambiguity inherent in prescriptive job description. Such avoidance is, he argues, effectively achieved by first explicitly (prescriptively) stating that CEOs should take whatever professional action is required to achieve the board's defined strategic goals/Ends while also avoiding all actions that have been explicitly (proscriptively) declared off limits by the board.

Although an element in the statement above involves the prescription that while the CEO will achieve the strategic goals/Ends approved by the board, the heart of the responsibility-delegation process is defined in the negative statement that the CEO will "not violate any operational work restrictions the board puts in place." In this approach, all CEO actions to achieve the agency's strategic goals/Ends are permitted—unless they are forbidden.

Fundamentally, what the board is doing when it sets up its proscriptive statements (what Carver calls *executive limitations* and others call *operational boundaries*) is describing the scope of action allowed the CEO. The board is telling the CEO that he or she can carry out any administrative action to achieve the strategic goals/Ends—as long as the action does not exceed the board-defined limits or boundaries.

The language used in a proscriptive delegation strategy is negative; the board is telling the CEO what he or she is *not* allowed to do. Those who approach this language with a prescriptive orientation (where the language is positive and tells the CEO what he or she is supposed to do) are often uncomfortable because the negatives seem "unfriendly." The aim, however, is to be clear about the boundaries around the CEO's field of operational action while declaring that the CEO is perfectly free to take any action he or she wishes within those boundaries. As long as the CEO stays within those limits, there is total freedom to act.

Although board members frequently feel uncomfortable with negative, proscriptive language, it can be argued that such language is typical of our cultural rules. Nearly everyone is familiar with the parts of the Ten Commandments that begin with "Thou shalt not—"; indeed, much if not most of our society operates on a proscriptive basis. We are encouraged to seek a successful and comfortable life as long as we don't break any of the many, many laws we have passed in our legislatures. Sports are imbued with proscriptive practices: coaches and players are asked to win as many games as possible in any way they want—as long as they don't break any rules of the game. Carver's advice actually has a long history in our wider culture.

The board has the power to define the operational limits very broadly or very narrowly. An example of a very broadly defined limit might be, "The CEO may not carry out any action that is unethical, imprudent, or illegal." In contrast, a very narrowly defined limit might state, "The CEO may not sign any check for more than $100." The more broadly defined the limits, the more freedom of action is given to the CEO. When the board defines the limits more narrowly, it is in effect retaining more of the agency's operational decisions at the board level while allowing less independence of action for the CEO. The degree to which the board reserves decisions for itself tends to reflect the extent to which they trust the CEO to do the right thing, in the sense that he or she would make the same decision the board might. It is the responsibility of each board to determine how broadly or narrowly it is prepared to limit the freedom of action of the CEO.

Below is an example of an actual executive-limitation statement used in an agency. This particular statement describes how this board decided to define the scope of action allowed the agency's CEO with respect to those operational matters that concerned the financial health of the organization. Bear in mind that just because this particular agency chose to do things this way, it does not mean that this is the "best" or the "right" way to do it. In any case, the language used is as follows:

Financial Health Protection

With respect to the actual, ongoing condition of the organization's financial health, the chief executive officer may not cause or allow the development of fiscal jeopardy or a material deviation of actual expenditures from board priorities as established in Ends policies.

More particularly, he or she may not:

1. Expend more funds than have been received in the fiscal year to date, unless otherwise approved by the board.
2. Indebt the organization in an amount greater than can be repaid by otherwise unencumbered revenues within sixty days.
3. Allow cash to drop below the amount needed to settle payroll and debts in a timely manner.
4. Allow tax payments or other government-ordered payments or filings to be overdue or inaccurately filed.
5. Allow actual allocations to deviate materially from board priorities in Ends policies.

Notice that the limitation statement consists of two parts. The first is the declaration that the CEO is not to allow the fiscal health of the agency to be placed in jeopardy (not defined) or allow expenditures to deviate from actions required to achieve the agency's strategic goals/Ends. This statement, while relatively broad, is narrower than the very broad restriction offered earlier as an example: "The CEO will not carry out any action that is unethical, imprudent, or illegal."

The second part of the financial-health-limitation statement consists of five very particular limits. These more detailed limits essentially define what the board regards as jeopardy, which was undefined in the first, more general statement. This list of five says the CEO, on his or her own, may not: run an annual deficit, may not cause debts to be greater than what can be paid for within sixty days, allow cash to fall so low that payroll cannot be met, allow tax or government-required deadlines for payment to be missed, or allow the allocation of money to differ from that required by board-defined priorities.

We need to be clear. These are limits on the CEO's activities. The board, if it so wishes, can approve limited-time violations of each of the limits. Or the board can change its mind, become more restrictive, and make operational decisions itself. Essentially, the board can reserve for itself the power to do these things. To this extent, the board can become more involved in operational matters. Whether it is wise to routinely do so is another matter entirely.

Let's look at a second and slightly more complex example of executive action limits; such complexities are not uncommon.

CEO-Board Communications

The chief executive officer may not fail to inform the board of matters that hinder the continuing effective operation of the agency.

More particularly, he or she may not:

1. Fail to advise the board of relevant issues, trends, material external and internal changes, and particularly changes in the assumptions upon which any board policy has previously been established when any of these reasonably ought to have been known by the CEO.
2. Fail to submit the required monitoring data (see policy on Monitoring Executive Performance) in a timely, accurate, and understandable fashion.
3. Fail to marshal as many staff and external points of view, issues, and options as are reasonably needed for informed board choices.

4. Present information in unnecessarily complex or lengthy form.

5. Fail to provide a mechanism for official board, officer, or committee communications.

6. Fail to deal with the board as a whole except when
   a. Fulfilling individual requests for information as specified in the Board-CEO linkage policy.
   b. Responding to officers or committees duly charged by the board.

7. Fail to report in a timely manner on actual or anticipated noncompliance with any policy of the board.

Again, the statement consists of two parts: a more generally stated component and a set of particulars that define more closely the main concerns of the board with respect to the communications the board expects from the CEO. This time, however, the limitation statement includes three levels of detail instead of two as in the earlier example. Component 6 has two subcomponents (a and b, above) which specify conditions under which the CEO is exempted from complying with the overall requirement of the component, which states that the CEO must always deal with the board as a whole (as opposed to responding to expectations and requests from individuals on the board or board committees). This sequencing of limitations, beginning with broad statements, progressing toward increasing degrees of narrowness, is typical of the proscriptive approach to responsibility delegation.

It will be immediately obvious that each one of these proscriptive/ negative statements can be turned around and expressed as prescriptive/ positive statements. It might be argued that in doing so, just what it is that the CEO is supposed to be doing becomes clearer. However, such a change in language reintroduces the problem of what to do with all those actions that are not listed/prescribed. Carver argues, with some merit, that the proscriptive language provides the CEO with considerably more freedom for independent action and removes from the situation any sense that there will be operational matters that might or might not need prior board approval. To restate a basic point, the essence of the proscriptive strategy is that if an action is not explicitly forbidden, it is permitted.

Maintaining the Delegation Arrangement

It is one thing to develop and adopt delegation policies for CEOs, but continuing to abide by the arrangement is another thing entirely. This is true whether the board uses a prescriptive job description approach or a proscriptive executive-limitation approach. Constant vigilance is required from both board and CEO if the responsibility assignment boundaries are to be respected. Pressures continually emerge to pull and push boards into taking on operational roles that they have previously delegated to the CEO.

There is absolutely nothing wrong with the board asking questions about a particular operational action or administrative procedure. Boards have the right to know everything. Moreover, there should be and usually are mechanisms consistent with the board's governance approach that empower it to have an indirect impact on operational matters. I will return to this topic in the next chapter.

The issue here goes beyond the board merely knowing about agency operations. A whole host of forces external to the agency and internal to the board's own inclinations frequently combine to tempt boards into taking decisions and passing motions that essentially usurp what has been deemed to be the CEO's responsibility domain. Let's consider some of the ways in which boards can be pulled into taking action on previously delegated operational matters.

Temptations due to requirements from external bodies:

- Funders require the signature of the board chair (which implies a board-level discussion and approval decision) on operational documents for which responsibility has been delegated to the CEO or for spending requests that are within the CEO's approved spending limit.

- Accreditation bodies require board motions approving operational policies that have been delegated to the CEO for development.
- Legislation, regulation, or licensing may require board approval for particular operational matters that the board has delegated to the CEO.

Temptations due to issues internal to the agency and the board:

- Some board members might disagree with an operational decision or action taken by the CEO.
- Board members might hear from staff members or clients that they are unhappy with something about the agency's operations.
- A board member might get a good idea for some sort of new practice that could be used in the agency.
- The CEO brings an operational matter to the board for discussion without being clear that the intent is to seek board advice, not approval/direction for action.

Each one of these enticements needs to be dealt with in some appropriate way. They should not be ignored; indeed, they often signal issues that will usually continue to grow and fester until they precipitate a crisis. Remember, at the end of the day, everything is the board's business, one way or another. How then should a board respond to these temptations? That depends on whether the temptation source is external or internal.

In many respects, dealing with temptations from external sources is easier. Consider the situation of a matter involving some CEO action, such as authorizing the expenditure of a modest sum of money that is within the CEO approval limits set by the board, but where the funder requires that there be formal board approval. The board could simply agree to pass a motion, without getting into a discussion about it. It could approve the expenditure so that board approval is formally acknowledged in the board minutes, or the board might simply pass a motion authorizing the board chair to sign a key form associated with the expenditure and the funder's requirement that there be a paper trail. The trick here is that the board should not find itself embroiled in a discussion of the substance of the decision. In other words, the board should not try to repeat the thinking-through process that the staff has already engaged in.

An increasingly frequent way of handling this situation is with the consent agenda,[9] which often comprises the initial part of the normal board agenda. The consent agenda includes all the items for board approval that do not require discussion. They are simply voted on as a block. It is through this mechanism that board approval is often recorded for staff-level policy decisions (as per the responsibility-delegation process that board has previously adopted) in order to meet accreditation or other regulatory requirements. This strategy helps boards stay away from the enticement to delve into the issues that have already been resolved at the staff level.[10]

Temptations to cross into delegated operational matters that arise from within the organization are more challenging. Frequently, the issue can have real ambiguity with respect to its status as either a board-governance matter or a staff-operational matter. In such cases, the board needs to have a clear-eyed sense of its responsibilities and its delegation policies.

---

9 See *The Consent Agenda: A Tool for Improving Governance* (Washington, DC: BoardSource, 2006) (www.boardsource.org).

10 Before calling for a vote on the consent agenda item, the chair must ask if any member would like an item on the consent agenda extracted and then placed on the regular agenda. This action opens the item to a full board discussion. This temptation, however, really should be resisted when it comes to operational items that are on the board agenda simply because an external body requires board approval.

When encountering one of these issues that might be an operational concern, the board should begin by simply asking itself if it should be dealing with the matter at all. The biggest danger is to simply assume that because the issue somehow got onto the board agenda that it really is a governance issue. If, after it reflects on the issue, the board concludes that the item is operational and not governance, it should refuse to deal with the matter and refer it back to the CEO for disposition.

Sometimes the CEO is responsible for an operational item getting onto the board agenda. For example, when faced with a difficult decision regarding a delegated responsibility, a CEO might wish to bring the matter to the board for resolution. A common context for this sort of temptation is the human-resources domain. Decisions on whom to hire rarely cause a CEO to bring the matter to the board for approval (though they will likely and properly do so for information as part of a regular board-report process). Decisions about employee dismissal are another matter. Because dismissal actions can be fraught with legal and/or personal risk, it is possible that a CEO might be uneasy about taking sole responsibility for such action. The CEO might feel more comfortable sharing liability for such action with the board and might bring the matter to the board table along with a motion to approve the dismissal. If such a motion is passed, it becomes a board action rather than a CEO/staff-level action.

Long ago, Carver[11] identified the CEO as a key agent for ensuring a strong maintenance of the governance work-operations work boundary. Board members come and go and vary enormously with respect to the amount of effort they are willing to put into learning good governance practices. CEOs, on the other hand, are there for the long haul and usually have a vested interest in ensuring that the governing habits of the board are at their most effective, including keeping them out of operational matters that have been delegated to the CEO. Here are some of

---

11 John Carver and Miriam Mayhew Carver, *The CEO Role Under Policy Governance* (A CarverGuide) (San Francisco: Jossey-Bass, 1997).

the key steps Carver urges CEOs to take. (I have paraphrased Carver's language here.)

- Don't invite the board to "overdefine" its strategic goals/Ends. Make sure that their definition is open enough for you to establish "any reasonable interpretation."
- Do not invite the board to comment on your plans; this can easily lead them into believing that they are being asked to approve the plans. Suppose you later want to change the plan. Can you do it without board approval?
- If you do consult board members on an issue, remember that it is you, not the board members, who bear responsibility for the decisions regarding operational matters.
- Carefully think about any information you give to the board; make sure it is germane to the policy achievements for which you are being held responsible. Do not give them extraneous information.

Carver's position on this issue is regarded by many as relatively extreme, but he does have a point. He insists that the board, and particularly the CEO, bear a significant responsibility to abide by the delegation of responsibility established by the board. The temptation to cross responsibility boundaries is often strong; therefore, a rigorous mindfulness is needed consistently to keep to the delegation agreement. Carver's recommendations certainly establish the clarity needed to keep most CEOs and boards out of trouble, but this strongly defined position comes with its own complications.

Primarily with Carver's position in mind, Chait, Ryan, and Taylor have argued that being too clear about board/governance vs. staff/operations boundaries might be problematic. They worry that by keeping board and staff apart, capacity for effective work is weakened. They wrote:

But the board-improvement approaches that do promise preci-
sion, with specific and fixed roles for trustees and staff, usually
involve a huge and generally unfavorable trade-off: more clarity
but less governance, comfort at the cost of impact. Such neat di-
visions of labor succeed by *relieving* boards and staff of the challenge of working together on important issues. Few partnerships,
none less than trustees and their chief executive, succeed on the
strength of clear boundaries. When trustees and staff share the
labor, the complexity of board-staff interactions are not elimi-
nated. But the results do make the tensions worth bearing (99).[12]

Chait, Ryan, and Taylor use the phrase, "more clarity but less governance" quite deliberately because they push for more collaborative effort between board and staff than seems to be the case with Carver's
position. Their view is that by combining the knowledge of both board
and staff, more expertise is harnessed in the task of developing strategic
goals/Ends for the agency. They have a point, but then so does Carver.
Clearly, we are at the nub of the problem. What are a board and a CEO
to do?

In my view, the wisest course for a board and a CEO is to stay focused
on the type of work involved (governance or operations) and on who
has responsibility for the work. It is entirely possible for the board to
benefit from the CEO's advice when formulating its policy positions. It is
also possible for the CEO to entertain the view of the board when working out operational plans or actions, but both sides have to be careful
when they consult the other. They have to keep asking themselves whose
responsibility it is to do the work. If they can pull it off, the board can
achieve the level of governance achievement Chait, Ryan, and Taylor
termed *generative governance*. This collaborative effort by board and staff
may find its finest expression when the board struggles to develop its

---

12 R. P. Chait, W. P. Ryan, and B. E. Taylor, *Governance as Leadership: Reframing
the Work of Nonprofit Boards* (Hoboken, NJ: John Wiley & Sons, 2004).

strategic goals/Ends and the staff develops operational plans intended to achieve those strategic goals/Ends. It is to this issue that I now turn.

The Strategic Plan Revisited

To reiterate, the traditional strategic plan is actually comprised of two separate although linked components: a set of strategic goals/Ends and an operational plan that describes how agency services will be delivered in order to achieve the strategic goals/Ends. Because the traditional strategic-planning exercise typically intertwines both a board component (strategic goals/Ends) and a staff component (operational plan), work on strategic plans offers many opportunities for boards and staffs to cross over into one another's responsibility domains. Most of the time, however, these crossings involve the board intruding into staff-delegated operations, rather than the reverse.

Strategic plans are often developed when the board and staff set aside a common retreat day to focus for an extended number of hours on defining the agency's strategic goals/Ends and on laying out the service procedures that should achieve the goals. The board, in a subsequent regular board meeting, commonly passes a motion giving the plan its formal approval. In effect, the board has determined the strategic goals/Ends (as it should), but it has also taken formal ownership of the operational plan that might be better left as a responsibility in the hands of the staff with the service expertise.

If the board has *not* previously and formally delegated operations work to the CEO, an approach where the board is the dominant party can work well enough, although the potential for subsequent role confusion can still result. Board approval means that the board-approved plan is to be the plan the CEO carries out; it is the board's plan, even though it was jointly developed. The implication is that only the board can change the plan, and that is done only via a board motion. If the CEO later feels he or she should do something different, the board really needs to approve any change.

The board, on the other hand, might have adopted a clear policy of delegating most operational matters to the CEO. Then, when it passes a motion approving the strategic plan as developed at the joint retreat day, it assumes ownership of the plan. This constitutes a contradiction in at least some of its delegation intentions. On the one hand, the board has given operational control (within defined limits) to the CEO, but it then decides that the service operations outlined in the board-approved strategic plan are the ones that must be implemented. In effect, the power to decide on service activities has been taken over by the board. The status of the CEO's power to freely act under the delegation policy is thereby compromised.

Does this mean the board should have no input into the operational plan component? Does it mean the board should make no formal decision regarding the operational plan? In my view, the answer to both of these questions is *no.* It is useful and maybe wise for the board (or some of the board members) to participate with the staff when the staff works on developing the operational plan that will specify how the strategic goals/Ends will be achieved. This is precisely the nexus of the Chait, Ryan, and Taylor position on generative governance. They argue that by bringing the creative talents of board *and* staff to the task, better work will be done. In the process, though, the participants should bear in mind that delegated operations work is best determined by the staff members who have the appropriate expertise even as they consider the advice from the board. In the end, the CEO should bear the responsibility for the plan's content.

This brings us to the question of what sort of decision the board should make regarding the operational component of the strategic plan. What can the board do? How can the board express its consent that the plan should/can be implemented without assuming responsibility for the plan?

Here the answer can begin to sound rather pedantic, but then most efforts to be careful in a tricky context share this challenge. At the very least, the board needs to show on the record that it has seen the plan, knows what is in it, and does not object to its contents. The best way to do this is to record a motion and show the result of a vote on the motion. What kind of motion can accomplish this without formally approving the plan (and thus take over ownership of it)?

I recommend that the board pass a motion saying something like, "The plan as presented is consistent with the agency's mission, vision, and values and is not inconsistent with what needs to be done to achieve the agency's strategic goals/Ends." This may strike some as a weak position for the board to take on such an important matter. The problem, as I have argued, is that in doing more (such as formally approving the plan), the CEO, to whom operations have been delegated, loses formal control of the plan; he or she can no longer feel fully free to modify the plan without board approval. Of course, the board can approve the plan, informally loosen its hold on the plan, and let the CEO make whatever changes are deemed necessary. At best, this leaves the situation in an ambiguous state. The CEO is exposed to the possibility that the board might unexpectedly retake control of what is really, in a formal sense, the board's plan. The likelihood of this happening is increased if the board disagrees with something that the CEO, in his or her professional wisdom, wishes to do.

However the board resolves the question of what to do with the operational plan, it cannot escape its accountability; it must know and understand what is being done operationally. This points to the board's responsibility to monitor, which is the focus of the next chapter.

5

Monitoring Staff Operations

IN ORDER FOR the board to satisfy its accountability requirements and carry out its responsibilities, it must have a steady inflow of relevant, high-quality information both from outside the agency as well as from the inside. When it formulates its strategic goals/Ends, the board relies significantly on information about the community external to the agency. Although board members bring their own community knowledge to the board table, the board must also plan for regular board education sessions wherein agency staff or other persons from the community make presentations to the board about matters of key importance to agency services.

The board's need for information, however, does not stop with the external sources that enable it to write its strategic goal/Ends statements. Of equal importance is the flow of information toward the board table from within the agency, so that the board can be assured that the CEO is properly carrying out delegated responsibilities and that the agency's strategic goals/Ends are being achieved. The use of such information internal to the agency is known as monitoring and is a critical board responsibility.

Carver has pointed out that there are three methods of gathering monitoring information: executive reports, external audits, and direct inspections by the board.

Executive reports are really reports by the CEO to the board that are normally given at some point during each board meeting. Such reports have a long tradition in the not-for-profit sector. Traditional CEO reports, however, can sometimes be a cause of unease among board members, because the CEO usually has nearly full control over what the board will be told. Happily, there are ways for the board to influence report content that will strengthen its confidence in the information the reports contain. I will turn to this issue shortly.

External financial audits are the second usual source of board information regarding internal operations. There is a very long tradition (and indeed, a requirement) under the legislation concerning legally established not-for-profit corporations that they conduct an annual third-party audit of agency finances. Many organizations are also subject to periodic accreditation reviews. Further, there is also nothing to stop boards from initiating ad hoc external operational reviews of their agencies anytime they wish, although such reviews are not usually a routine part of ongoing operations-monitoring arrangements.

Carver's third source of information for the board is from what he termed *direct inspections,* where the board initiates a review carried out by one or more members of the board of some component of the agency's operations. Direct inspections can be difficult processes to manage because they might lead boards to cross the boundary line between governance work and delegated operations. Moreover, board members often do not possess the expertise required to conduct such inspections. On the other hand, if the inspections are mainly limited to verifying that key documents are being properly maintained and secured or that other easily verified routine procedures are being followed as required by agency policy or the law, direct inspections can work well.

Of these three methods of obtaining monitoring information, by far the most extensively used and relied on is the executive report, wherein the CEO regularly and frequently informs the board of what it needs to know. Financial audits are normally done only once a year. Accreditation reviews, should they happen at all, are performed at three-, four-, or five-year intervals. Direct inspections by the board, beyond checking routine matters, are rare. These are typically seen only when the board becomes aware of a need for extraordinary measures. For better or worse, the board typically has to rely on the CEO to keep it informed of the agency's operations, the risks that might threaten the agency, and the progress the agency is making in achieving its purposes.

Making the Executive Report More Effective

In some ways, it is ironic that the CEO determines the majority of the monitoring information the board receives. By tradition, the CEO prepares a written report for each board meeting, where the CEO will inform the board of all key agency developments that have transpired since the last executive report. What the board receives is almost entirely at the sole discretion of the CEO, and anything the CEO wishes to conceal from the board or not talk about can be left out. Of course, too much of this sort of leaving-out will probably not work in the long run if the information omitted is critical or significant. Bad news has a way of eventually making itself known. In the meantime, all manner of damage to the agency can happen.

Let's be clear here: CEOs are almost always honest, professional people who manage their relationships with their boards in open and transparent ways. Even when CEOs fail to report critical information to their boards, it is not usually with malice aforethought. Sometimes they just don't see that the information is critical or they want to avoid having to admit to what they believe is a minor mistake they hope will simply go away. Although it happens, most of the time boards do not have to worry too much about fraud and malfeasance.

Getting around the CEO-information-control problem is really quite simple: the board needs to tell the CEO clearly what it wants to see in the executive reports. This way, the board retains more control over the information it receives from the staff and increases the likelihood that the CEO self-reports will contain important and critical information. However, being clear with the CEO about what to report requires effort, clarity, and discipline on the board's part, and, of course, this strategy cannot guarantee that a CEO who wants to hide something from the board will be prevented from doing so. This is why third-party reports and direct inspections must be retained as possible monitoring devices.

The effectiveness of the board's monitoring is greatly enhanced if the board takes primary responsibility for determining what sorts of information are to be included in the CEO's executive reports. The board can take control by developing policies regarding what it wants to see in CEO reports and how frequently.

In framing its executive reporting specifications with respect to the operational work assigned to the CEO, the board can turn to its articles of delegation for guidance. If the traditional job description is being used in an agency to define what is delegated to the CEO, the board can identify the main operational categories in the job description and ask the CEO to report any significant agency activity within the categories. The board might further specify that each of the main components of the job description be reported on at least annually, to ensure that the board receives information on each of the key operations from time to time.

Boards that have elected to follow Carver's advice and use executive-limitation policies to specify the delegation of operational responsibilities can require that the CEO report on each area of delegation and even on each of the specific components within the broader operational areas. Where the traditional job description is usually written in very general language, executive-limitation statements can be very specific. If the board receives a report on each of these at least annually, it will have a very clear idea of how the CEO is managing his or her responsibilities.

Exhibit 1 offers an example of how an executive-limitations-monitoring report might be written by a CEO. This particular example is a slightly modified version of a monitoring report from an actual agency, although I have taken care to remove all identifying information. In this particular example of a financial conditions executive limitation, the monitoring report repeats the board-approved executive-limitation policy language at the top and in the left-hand column. As Carver advises, the CEO has inserted her interpretation, in positive language, of what she sees as the intent of the board. If the board does not accept the CEO's interpretation, it can ask the CEO to change it. It might also change the language in its executive-limitation policy to make the board's intent clearer.

The key monitoring information is contained in the center column of the table, where the CEO describes what she has done to ensure compliance with the policy. In the third column, the CEO can place a check mark to indicate that she has complied with the policy. The board's task on receiving this report is to either accept or reject the CEO's claim of compliance. A failure to comply could constitute a performance failure to be noted at the time of the periodic performance evaluation; it might also signal a problem with the policy that precipitates some sort of change in the policy language itself.

Exhibit 1

Executive Limitations Financial: Financial Condition

General CEO Constraint: The CEO shall not cause or allow any practice, activity, decision, or organizational circumstance which is illegal, imprudent, or in violation of commonly accepted business practice and professional ethics.

Global Policy Statement

With respect to the actual, ongoing condition of the organization's financial health, the CEO shall not cause or allow the development of fiscal jeopardy or a material deviation of actual expenditures from Board priorities established in Ends policies.

Further, the CEO shall not:	CEO Response	Comp
a. Expend more funds than have been received in the fiscal year to date unless the debt guideline below is met: - Indebt the organization in an amount greater than can be repaid by certain, otherwise unencumbered revenues within ninety days. CEO Interpretation Funds are expended according to revenue projections for each fiscal year, and the agency is not indebted beyond what can be repaid within sixty days.	The only debt that we take on is for our credit card accounts, which are paid up by the due date every month.	
b. Fail to maintain an internally restricted fund for contingencies of $65,000, or such other amount as set by the board; at any given time, should cash flow require encroaching on this fund, the board will be informed at its next meeting and the fund will be restored in a timely manner. CEO Interpretation The contingency fund is maintained as approved by the board. If it should be depleted, it is restored within fiscal year end.	The contingency fund is currently set by the board at $59,033 (as per the last audited financial statements). To formalize the increase to $65,000, the board should pass a motion to increase this fund to $65,000.00. There are unallocated surplus funds ($40,987 as per the last audited financial statements) being held by the agency, which would allow for increasing the fund to this amount.	
d. Allow debts to be paid in an untimely manner. CEO Interpretation Debts/invoices are paid within one month, unless there is a dispute about the	All invoices are paid within thirty days unless there is a dispute about the invoice.	

Further, the CEO shall not:	CEO Response	Comp
invoice or other unusual circumstances.		
e. Allow the collection of accounts receivable to be undertaken in an untimely manner. CEO Interpretation Collection of accounts receivable in an untimely manner means beyond ninety days.	Accounts receivable have been collected within ninety days of the due date (invoices allow a sixty-day payment period and email/phone reminders are made after this date, to ensure that all accounts owing are collected.)	
f. Allow tax payments or other government-ordered payments or filings to be overdue or inaccurately filed. CEO Interpretation Ensure that all payments are made as required with no penalties charged.	- Government forms (e.g., T3010) and receiver general payments have been submitted on time.	
g. Allow agency credit cards to be used for anything other than business-related expenses, nor allow more than two agency business credit cards that have higher than the following spending limits: CEO credit card to have a spending limit no higher than $15,000.00 and the administrative coordinator credit card to have a spending limit of no higher than $1,000.00. CEO Interpretation Create and enforce an operational policy that complies with these limitations on agency credit cards.	- There are only two agency business credit cards and these are allocated according to this policy. The treasurer (or another board signing officer, if the treasurer is not available) signs off on the CEO's credit card statements. - Agency financial policies include these limitations.	
h. Allow the accrual of any employee benefits such as sick time, lieu time, or vacation time that would cause an imprudent liability. CEO Interpretation Create and enforce an operational policy with limitations on the accumulation of sick, holiday, and flex or	Agency HR policy allows a max accumulation of fifteen sick days and carryover to next fiscal year, of a max of ten vacation days. Overtime may be incurred, but has never been approved. Flex time is allowed if approved, up to a maximum of seventy hours, and, if earned, must be taken back on a regular basis. As of the last fiscal year, no employee had	

Further, the CEO shall not:	CEO Response	Comp
overtime (policy described in right-hand column).	accumulated more than these amounts. The agency also has a supplemental parental leave plan for permanent staff who have been with the agency for at least twenty-four months. The agency pays employee on leave 25 percent of her gross salary for up to six months of leave. No one is currently on maternity leave.	

If the board asks the CEO to prepare one or more such reports on executive-limitation policies for each board meeting, the whole set of executive-limitation policies will have been reported on over the course of the board year. Indeed, the wise board will establish a yearlong schedule of such reports. This process ensures that the board will receive fairly detailed accounts of how the CEO is complying or not complying with board policies.

While a once-a-year monitoring report is probably sufficient for most agency operations, some require more frequent reporting because of their operational significance. Key among these critical operational areas are: finances and risk.

Monitoring the Agency's Financial/Fiscal Health

Agency finances are one of the most significant areas of risk for boards. As such, a good grasp of the financial health of the agency is important if board confidence is to be sustained. A wise board will ask the CEO to report on agency finances at least quarterly, if not at each board meeting. In the report, the CEO should be asked to explain any unexpected significant deviations from planned budgetary expenditures and to offer a plan for how the deviation can be corrected.

Monitoring Agency Risk Conditions

It is also reasonable for the board to ask the CEO to report on any significant risks or threats, both internal and external, to the agency's operations and sustainability at each board meeting. There might be staffing issues that could lead to lawsuits, or there might be policy changes by funders that could threaten agency viability. The board needs to know about these sorts of things so that it can develop a policy response, should one become necessary.

Different Forms of Information

Once a board has made it clear that it wants periodic reports on the key areas of operational delegation along with financial and risk conditions at specified frequencies, the major areas of concern for that board are pretty much covered. Nevertheless, there may be other matters on which the board may wish to receive information from the CEO. Such information can often help the board develop a more robust understanding of the context for agency operations and result in better planning and the definition of future strategic goals/Ends.

There is a danger, however, for the board in seeking out nebulously defined information beyond what is needed to effectively monitor the agency's (and CEO's) operational performance and goal achievement. Such information can tempt the board to cross the line between its own legitimate sphere of responsibility and the sphere that it has delegated to the CEO. A wise board will exercise caution here. Carver has developed a useful distinction between what he calls *monitoring information* and *incidental information*.

By Carver's definition, monitoring information is any content from the executive and other reports that is directly concerned with operational matters delegated to the CEO. Such information bears strongly on the performance of the CEO and, by extension, the whole agency. As previously discussed, the board has a responsibility to know about these things and to seek assurances that all is well. All executive reports focused on executive limitations constitute monitoring information. All reports on the degree to which strategic goals/Ends are being achieved contain key monitoring information.

Incidental information is all other information. If the information is not directly and explicitly linked to any criteria the board can use to measure performance, then it is deemed to be incidental. The board should regard it as background information, even though it might help the board members to better understand issues and might be useful for future planning. Ironically, for many board members, this incidental information can be the most interesting information they receive at the board table. As such, they may be tempted to become active in any associated operational matters, but this temptation should be resisted.

6

Monitoring Strategic Goal/
Ends Achievement

THE BOARD SHOULD expect to receive a report from the CEO at least annually on the degree to which the board-defined strategic goals/Ends have been achieved. Yet, ironically, this particular activity is not very often carried out in any form at all in not-for-profit agencies. Instead, boards mostly see data on service-delivery activity. Ultimately, the responsibility for this failure rests with the board. It is the board's job to specify the strategic goals/Ends to be achieved, and the board must require the CEO to report periodically on the degree to which the strategic goals/Ends have indeed been achieved.

What we have here is one of those situations where it is easier to *say* what should be done than it is actually *do* what should be done. It is important for all board members—especially new ones—to understand the nature of this challenge and to appreciate the difficulties inherent in carrying out this aspect of their board responsibility.

The last twenty years or do have seen a general rise in the search for evidence of service impacts. Such information is now commonly available in business and industry where service or production objectives are usually more readily defined and assessed. If a plumber does poor work, the pipes will leak and the toilets will not flush properly. If cars or light bulbs are poorly built, they will not work properly. The buying public will not be repeat buyers, and the business will soon cease to exist. If people die in unusually large numbers when undergoing a particular surgical intervention, the surgeons cease using that technique. Knowledge of the relationship between service activities and the key outcomes is critical.

At the heart of continuous quality-improvement programs is a strong focus on the quality of the products produced. When manufacturing errors are detected, a great deal of attention is directed at product weaknesses, so that the source of the errors in the production process can be identified and fixed. Again, the value of an outcomes orientation is evident.

Given the clear benefits accruing to outcomes measurement in the business/industrial world, it is no surprise that there has been increasing pressure on agencies offering social services to demonstrate service-impact effects. Government and other funders are now more likely to ask for evidence that the monies they provide to support services actually lead to the kinds of outcomes claimed in agency funding applications. Increasingly, board members who come from the business world are puzzled about the general lack of attention to an outcomes orientation in the not-for-profit world.

So, what's the problem? Why has the not-for-profit service sector not more vigorously taken up the use of outcomes approaches to operations and management? As I have already indicated, it is inherently difficult to follow an outcomes orientation in community-based human services, particularly those that are social in nature. Being clear about expected service outcomes when those outcomes involve social processes is more challenging than when car engines or light bulbs are involved. If board members are to deal with such challenges successfully, they need to have a good grasp of them and be aware of how they make the task of outcomes assessment considerably more complex.

Critical Role of the Board

As is always the case in not-for-profit agencies, the responsibility for ensuring that agency strategic goals/Ends (as client outcomes) are achieved begins with the board, but success depends on whether or not the CEO and staff carry out service actions that are linked to specified outcomes. The board must establish the appropriate initial policies and then take responsibility for insisting that the CEO and the staff operate in ways consistent with the policies. If a true outcomes orientation is to be followed, there are several steps that begin with the board and then cascade down through the organization as first the board and then the staff do their assigned work.

Step 1. The board defines its strategic goals/Ends using outcomes language, as described in chapter 3.

Step 2. The board adopts appropriate CEO delegation policies, including the expectation that the CEO will ensure that the strategic goals/Ends will be achieved. The articles of delegation might be in the form of the traditional job descriptions (in spite of their inherent problems) or in the form of executive-limitation policies that are favored by Carver's Policy Governance boards. While boards can reserve to themselves the authority to define precisely the indicators of goal/Ends achievement, the wise board will leave the fine-grained detail of indicator measurement to the CEO and the professional staff. If it leaves the detailed indicators to the CEO, then it should explicitly state that the board must be satisfied with the CEO's reasonable interpretations of the board's more generally stated strategic goals/Ends.

Step 3. The board adopts a formal monitoring policy and procedures that require the CEO to periodically report to the board on the degree to which the agency's strategic goals/Ends are being achieved, as demonstrated by service-impact indicators.

Step 4. The board adopts a policy of regarding the strategic goals/Ends achievement monitoring reports as part of the CEO's periodic performance appraisals.

Step 5. The board adopts a formal commitment to consider the CEO's reported strategic goal/Ends achievement data when it conducts its periodic (preferably annual) review of the agency's strategic goals/Ends.

Each one of these steps is critically important, and none can be skipped if an outcomes orientation is to be followed. Given the complexity of processes that need to be in place, there are plenty of places along the way for operational failure. The board might not express its strategic goals/Ends in outcomes language. The board may fail to specify well enough what it wishes the CEO to achieve in its delegation policies, or the board may fail to insist that the CEO offer reasonable interpretations of what its broadly stated strategic goals/Ends actually mean in concrete terms. Further, the board may not require the CEO to provide regular strategic goal/Ends monitoring reports, particularly if the board does not regard such reports as a formal part of the CEO's performance evaluation. Adopting a policy that is not enforced is often no better than not adopting one in the first place.

Measurement: The Final Achilles Heel of Assessing Outcomes

Suppose the board manages to both formulate all of the policies required to induce the development of service-outcome indicators and develop procedures to support CEO reporting on outcomes achievement. Further suppose that the CEO manages to reasonably interpret board-stated strategic goals/Ends and defines acceptable outcome in-dictors. Even after all of this, a major challenge remains: how is the CEO actually to measure the outcome indicators? This is not an easy question to answer.

When it comes to the anticipated outcomes for most not-for-profit agencies offering social and health services, the indicators are almost always phenomena that can either be counted or rated. Countable out-comes are the easiest and least ambiguous to work with. The YMCA/YWCA might offer swimming lessons and, as an outcome, might count the number of five- and six-year-old children who can swim five lengths in the pool. A credit-counseling agency might count the number of debts that are fully paid. A marriage-counseling service might count the fre-quency of serious marital disputes per month. A parent-education ser-vice might count the frequency of child temper tantrums. If the boards of these agencies accept these indicators as reasonable interpretation of their board-approved strategic goals/Ends, then they can readily see that the services being provided by the staff of the agency are achieving the expected results.

Unfortunately for many (if not most) not-for-profit agency services, the anticipated outcomes are not countable ones. Many services are di-rected at changes in clients that can only be measured by some sort of rating system. If an agency intervention is aimed at helping people deal with depression, about the only method of measurement available is a depression-rating scale. It is the same with any intervention goal that depends on objective measurement of the mental and physical health of their clients, a factor that is not easily measured objectively. Moreover, such interventions are aimed at life circumstances that are unique to each person. No standard way of measuring changes in such conditions exists or is likely to exist. While theoretically possible, devising outcome measures for social and psychological phenomena that are tightly linked to intervention strategies is fraught with conceptual and technological difficulties.

What about Using Client Satisfaction Surveys?

Probably the most frequently seen outcome measure in not-for-profit agencies is the universal client satisfaction survey. Such surveys are, of course, worthy undertakings, but in the end, they provide the board with little evidence of intervention impacts. Typically, the returns on these surveys are depressingly low, somewhere in the neighborhood of 15 to 20 percent. A board is very likely to look for more. Client satisfaction is not normally a strategic goal/End that the board regards as a primary aim for the agency. To be sure, it is nice that clients are satisfied, but are their problems solved? That is the question.

Still, all is not lost. If the CEO is focused on continuous quality improvement, then negative feedback from client surveys is an excellent source of information when the aim is to identify the service components that are not meeting with client approval. Such information can be invaluable in improving the quality of services. This, however, is not the same thing as having evidence that the strategic goals/Ends of the services are being achieved.

Should Boards Give Up on the Idea of Outcomes Assessment?

The answer to this question is simple: absolutely not! Just because it is a hard thing to do does not mean that boards and CEOs should give up trying to do it. If the board takes the required steps to develop the needed policies and procedures and then requires the CEO to do the work at the staff level, over time any agency can gradually move to an outcomes-based assessment of service-delivery impacts.

The enterprise will likely fail if the board and staff attempt to develop outcome measures for all agency services all at once. The job is just too big to be done quickly, and fatigue will set in long before any worthwhile payoff emerges. The probability is high that people will just give up on the plan; but if the board explicitly states that it is happy if the CEO can develop outcome indicators and measures, for even a few of the potentially dozens of outcomes that flow from the typical social- or health-service agency, progress will happen. Over time, the work can be extended to cover more outcomes. Success can be possible.

7

Monitoring Board Operations

A WELL-FUNCTIONING BOARD not only has to make itself aware of how the CEO and the agency are operating, it must also assure itself that its governance practices are also up to standards. Too often, boards work hard to understand and question the work done by staff without also turning a critical eye on their own activities as governors. There is never a good reason for boards to remain blind to the quality of their own work.

The Chief Governance Officer

A good starting point for boards is the formal designation of one of their number to act as the guardian of governance matters. Carver refers to this person as the chief governance officer (CGO). This person's role is to take the lead in ensuring that the board is diligent in respecting its own policies and declarations of purpose. Often, this modest policing role falls to the board chair or president. It might also be the past chair or past president who might, as is often the case, be serving as chair of the nominating committee or governance committee, the latter coming to be the preferred term.

A good governance minder will be very knowledgeable about the board's approved governance policies and will understand what they mean in terms of concrete board action. Whenever the board does not follow its own rules or fails to respect the boundaries of delegated power, the CGO will remind the board of its agreed-upon obligations and signal when the board needs to proceed more appropriately. However, leaving it as the sole responsibility of a senior board member is not really adequate; monitoring for good governance practices ought to be a shared task.

General Board Mindfulness

If a board is determined to perform its duties responsibly, then it should expect every board member to be constantly mindful of how the board collectively does its work and whether it remains faithful to its governance policies—or fails to do so. It is too easy to drift away from these policies for all of the tempting reasons explored in chapter 4. Each member of the board has the responsibility to be vigilant in observing appropriate board behavior. Not only should board members be scrupulous with respect to their ethics, but they also have an obligation to operate according to the governance policies they adopt.

As I have shown, there are many forces that pressure boards to step over the delegation boundary into operations work that has been delegated to the CEO. While it helps to rely on the designated governance minder, it is much better if all board members become conscious of the way they approach those operational matters that are the province of the CEO. The question that should be foremost and consistently in the minds of the board members is clear: what role does the board have to play in regard to the issue under discussion? If they find themselves about to make a decision that they have previously delegated to the CEO, they should immediately cease discussion and move on to another topic. There is nothing wrong with knowing about and understanding the issue the CEO is dealing with, but the board needs to consider the wisdom of delving into operational decision making. Knowing about an issue is acceptable (and maybe even desirable), but taking over a delegated operational decision is not. This is something for all board members to keep in mind all the time.

Annualized Board Performance Monitoring

Relying on a designated governance officer and general board mindfulness is fine, but it is likely not enough to ensure that the board remains disciplined in its approach to governance; such rigorous mindfulness is not easily sustained. Consequently, it is also helpful for the board to engage in some more objective questioning of its own behavior. By formalizing the performance assessment with survey instruments, the board is more likely to focus on the key requirements of good board practice. The frequency with which these surveys happen is important.

At the very least, the board should conduct an annual self-survey to ensure that the board members see that they have adhered to board practices that are consistent with the board's own policies. Survey questionnaires frequently used by boards in such situations are easily found on the Internet. Below is a list of twenty statements that have proved useful in board self-evaluations. Board members are asked to respond to each statement by indicating if they agree, disagree, or are unsure as to how to respond. They are also invited to provide a comment on each question. When responses indicate poor board performance, comments are particularly helpful in identifying ways to improve.

1. The organization's vision, direction, and objectives are understood and supported by all board members.
2. The board is clear on the direction the organization should be taking and annually reviews the vision and values to ensure they remain relevant.

3. The board collectively reviews the organization's strategic goals/Ends policy annually.

4. The roles and responsibilities of the board and the management team are clearly defined and separated.

5. Board members collectively have the right skill mix to effectively govern the organization.

6. The orientation given to new board members is effective in preparing them for their role as board members.

7. The board has a process in place for identifying, evaluating, and managing risk.

8. The board meets regularly and has agreed on the annual work plan.

9. The agenda and supporting papers are distributed in advance of the meetings, and members are well prepared.

10. The board chair runs the meetings effectively and keeps the board focused on the governance role of the board.

11. All board members are given the opportunity to participate, and different points of view are respected.

12. Minutes of all board meetings and major decisions are recorded.

13. The board's committees help to add value and improve the effectiveness of the full board.

14. The board's committees complete the tasks assigned to them effectively and report regularly to the board.

15. Each committee reviews its objectives, responsibilities, and terms of reference annually.

16. The board understands the community it seeks to serve.

17. The board ensures that any public funding it receives is used in ways consistent with its strategic goals/Ends.

18. The board ensures that the organization's objectives and accomplishments are communicated to the community.

19. The financial reports and financial status of the organization are understood by all board members.

20. Accurate financial reports are completed by a suitably qualified person on a regular basis.

This list of twenty items is not intended to be ideal or the best for all boards and agencies. Each board should develop its own self-evaluation questions to ensure that feedback is obtained on all key features deemed important by each board. There is no reason to limit responses to agree/ disagree. Any sort of scale of measurement can be used.

Another approach to an annual governance-practices-monitoring schedule is to combine it with an annual review of the content of board-governance policies (as described in chapter 3). Indeed, agency accreditation programs invariably require that boards provide evidence that they have, within a specified period of time, formally reviewed the content of their policies to ensure that they remain current and effective. When the policy content is reviewed, the board can also ask itself if it is actually operating in accordance with the policy. The benefits of this combined exercise can be considerable. Not only is the board assured that its policies are still current and appropriately representative of best practices, the additional step of asking if the board is actually following its own policies makes the monitoring process very efficient.

Boards that conduct these sorts of combined review and monitoring procedures typically do so on an annual basis with respect to each of their governance-policy statements. If a board has a dozen or so separate governance-policy statements, each dealing with a separate governance domain, they might ask each board member to take one or two of the policies and lead the board through a formal review process. There will be a brief consideration at the board table of whether the policy statement is still current and adequate, as well as how well the board is following the requirements of the policy. If one or two policies are considered in this fashion in each board meeting through the year, every policy gets reviewed annually, and the board is constantly faced with its own performance adequacy.

More Frequent Monitoring

Carver, while seeing value in these annual questionnaires and monitoring exercises, suggests that if a board is genuinely interested in remaining faithful to its policies and to correcting errors, a more frequent check on process is useful. Some boards might do such a self-check quarterly; others might take a few minutes at the end of each board meeting to discuss if the board followed acceptable practices during the meeting. The advantage of more frequent surveys is that continuous mindfulness is more likely to occur.

Below is a list of questions that the board can ask itself at the end of each meeting or at the end of every third or fourth meeting. This list happens to consist of nine questions, but it could be fewer or more. The number of questions and their content really should be a function of the particular governing style of any given agency. Typically, the board secretary reads the question, and the board members collectively declare their response (but not one at a time, of course). By the end of the meeting, everyone wants to go home. There might be a brief discussion about what the correct response should be, but usually there is ready agreement around the table. If the board as a whole agrees that it has done the right thing, a check mark is entered into a chart by the secretary to accumulate a record of how the board sees itself doing over the course of the board year. Bear in mind that not every item on the list is dealt with in every meeting. At year's end, the record can be examined for critical gaps, to see if the board is systematically missing out on some key governance tasks.

1. Did the board meeting agenda deal with the issues required by the board calendar?
2. Did the discussion during the board meeting adhere to the principles of the approved governance model?
3. Did the board educate itself about the community it serves?
4. Did the board educate itself about services offered by the agency?
5. Did the board receive and consider a risk-analysis report from staff?
6. Did the board receive and consider a monitoring report in accordance with its approved monitoring schedule?

7. Were the service or operational matters presented to the board by staff assessed with respect to their consistency with the board's approved vision, mission, values, and strategic goals/Ends for the agency?

8. Did the board ensure itself that the finances of the agency were within acceptable limits?

9. Did the board address all issues and documents that require board approval?

If, during the self-monitoring, a performance deficiency is noticed, steps can then be taken to rectify the situation. This might require a revision of a policy or a renewal of a commitment to follow policy. It could also identify an area in which the board would benefit from more training. With such an eye on performance, board effectiveness and sophistication cannot help but increase.

8

Final Thoughts

As I SAID at the beginning, this short book is intended only as an orientation. There is a great deal more detail one can learn; the intricacies of governance practice in the real world can be complex. After all, we are talking about human social interactions, and such matters can be frustratingly nuanced, which creates significant ambiguity in the judgment process. Boards and board members will never make perfect decisions all the time. Errors will be made; lessons will be learned. There will even be disagreements over whether any errors have actually been made and whether there were indeed lessons to be learned. Be prepared to be tolerant and forgiving.

As you take up your board responsibilities, you really only need to keep a few basic ideas or principles in mind. Ask yourself how they apply to the situations that emerge during your board meetings.

What are these basic ideas?

1. The board is ultimately accountable to the "ownership" community for the kind of services provided by the agency and the way in which the services are offered.

2. The board has a continual obligation to learn about the community's evolving needs and how to use that information in determining the strategic goals/Ends of the agency.

3. The board needs to understand the differences between governance and the operational aspects of service delivery, as well as the relationship between the two.

4. The board should develop clearly stated policies regarding the delegation of responsibilities to the CEO.

5. Subsequently, the board must take care to respect the boundary between board and CEO responsibilities, as defined in the delegation policies.

6. The board should regularly monitor the way staff responsibilities are being carried out. It must be prepared to provide feedback to the CEO when operational responsibilities are not done in accordance with the board-determined strategic goals/Ends and the policies of delegation.

7. Finally, the board should monitor its own governing performance on a regular basis, to assure itself that it is acting in ways consistent with its own governance policies.

Of course, it helps in deciding how the principles apply if you do some more in-depth reading on governance and governance practices. Having more extensive knowledge of techniques makes it easier to take concrete action in real situations. I have provided more in-depth sources on the next page.

Additional Resources

FIRST, A COUPLE of excellent websites:

BoardSource.org: A rich source of information on board governance. They are based in Washington, DC.

policygovernance.com: This is the master website for any and all authoritative information on John Carver's Policy Governance Model. The site offers access to many publications and electronic materials.

Books on governance:

BoardSource. *Handbook of Nonprofit Governance.* San Francisco: Jossey-Bass, 2010.

Brown, J. *The Imperfect Board Member: Discovering the Seven Disciplines of Governance Excellence.* San Francisco: Jossey-Bass, 2006.

Carver, J. *Boards That Make a Difference: A New Design for Leadership in Nonprofit and Public Organizations.* San Francisco: Jossey-Bass, 2006.

Carver, J., and M. Carver. *Reinventing Your Board: A Step-by-Step Guide to Implementing Policy Governance.* San Francisco: Jossey-Bass, 2006.

Chait, R. P., W. P. Ryan, and B. E. Taylor. *Governance as Leadership: Reframing the Work of Nonprofit Boards.* Hoboken, NJ: John Wiley & Sons, 2004.

Laughlin, F. L., and R. C. Andringa. *Good Governance for Non-Profits: Developing Principles and Policies for an Effective Board.* New York: American Management Association, 2007.

About the Author

BRUCE A. RYAN, PhD, is Professor Emeritus of child and youth studies in the Department of Family Relations and Applied Nutrition at the University of Guelph.

Ryan has served as a member on many different boards. He was the president / board chair of Family Service Ontario, president of the Guelph Community Health Centre, board chair for the Canadian Centre Accreditation, and board chair for the accreditation committees for Family Service Ontario / Family Service Canada and for the Canadian Association of Credit Counseling Services.

Ryan has worked for thirty years as an on-site accreditation reviewer for family services across Canada. He specializes in agency governance practices.